JOE BIDEN
Making a Difference as President

By Katie Kawa

People Who Make a Difference

Published in 2023 by
KidHaven Publishing, an Imprint of Greenhaven Publishing, LLC
29 E. 21st Street
New York, NY 10010

Copyright © 2023 KidHaven Publishing, an Imprint of Greenhaven Publishing, LLC.

All rights reserved. No part of this book may be reproduced in any form without permission in writing from the publisher, except by a reviewer.

Designer: Deanna Paternostro
Editor: Katie Kawa

Photo credits: Cover lev radin/Shutterstock.com; pp. 5, 18 BiksuTong/Shutterstock.com; p. 7 Oliver Contreras/Sipa USA/AP Images; p. 9 Associated Press/AP Images; p. 11 mark reinstein/Shutterstock.com; p. 13 MediaPunch Inc/Alamy Stock Photo; p. 15 UPI/Alamy Stock Photo; p. 17 White House Photo/Alamy Stock Photo; p. 20 Spike Johnson/Shutterstock.com; p. 21 T.Sumaetho/Shutterstock.com.

Library of Congress Cataloging-in-Publication Data

Names: Kawa, Katie, author.
Title: Joe Biden : making a difference as president / Katie Kawa.
Description: New York : KidHaven Publishing, [2023] | Series: People who make a difference | Includes index.
Identifiers: LCCN 2022002921 | ISBN 9781534541788 (set) | ISBN 9781534541795 (library binding) | ISBN 9781534541771 (paperback) | ISBN 9781534541801 (ebook)
Subjects: LCSH: Biden, Joseph R., Jr.–Juvenile literature. | United States–Politics and government–1989–Juvenile literature. | Presidents–United States–Biography–Juvenile literature. | Politicians–United States–Biography–Juvenile literature. | Legislators–United States–Biography–Juvenile literature. | United States–Politics and government–1945-1989–Juvenile literature. | Delaware–Biography–Juvenile literature.
Classification: LCC E917 .K39 2023 | DDC 973.934092 [B]–dc23
LC record available at https://lccn.loc.gov/2022002921

Printed in the United States of America

CPSIA compliance information: Batch #CSKH23: For further information contact Greenhaven Publishing LLC, New York, New York at 1-844-317-7404.

Please visit our website, www.greenhavenpublishing.com. For a free color catalog of all our high-quality books, call toll free 1-844-317-7404 or fax 1-844-317-7405.

Find us on

CONTENTS

The Power of the Presidency	4
Schools Days	6
Highs and Lows	8
Family First	10
Mr. Vice President	12
Endings and Beginnings	14
Making History	16
Straight to Work	18
A Leader for Hard Times	20
Glossary	22
For More Information	23
Index	24

THE POWER OF THE PRESIDENCY

The president of the United States is able to make a very big difference—not just in the country they serve, but also around the world. They sign bills into law; appoint, or name, people to serve in government positions; and meet with other world leaders to fix problems and build a better future.

On January 20, 2021, Joseph R. Biden Jr. took on these **responsibilities** and more when he became the 46th president of the United States. Joe's journey to the White House was long and sometimes hard, but he never gave up. He kept going and learned important lessons along the way.

In His Words

"I believe the power of the presidency and the purpose is to unite this nation, not divide it; to lift us up, not tear us apart … Deep in the heart of America burns a flame lit almost 250 years ago—of liberty, freedom, and equality."

— Speech given on January 6, 2022

On January 20, 2021, Joe Biden took the oath of office—the promise all U.S. presidents make to serve their country. However, Joe had been serving his country in many ways long before taking that oath.

SCHOOL DAYS

Joe Biden's path to the presidency began in 1942. He was born on November 20 of that year and was the oldest of four siblings. Joe grew up in Scranton, Pennsylvania, but his family later moved to Delaware, which is where Joe would spend most of his life.

Joe went to college at the University of Delaware. He graduated, or finished school, in 1965. The next year, he married Neilia Hunter. Joe and Neilia got married while he was going to law school at Syracuse University in New York. He graduated from there in 1968 and began working as a **lawyer** back home in Delaware.

In His Words

"My mother's creed [belief] is the American creed: No one is better than you. You are everyone's equal, and everyone is equal to you."

— Speech given at the 2008 Democratic National Convention

Joe grew up with a stutter. This is a kind of speech disorder, which is a condition that makes it hard for someone to make the sounds they need to clearly speak to others. Joe worked hard to become a good public speaker. He **inspires** many people with speech disorders today, including Amanda Gorman (shown here), who read a poem she wrote at his **inauguration**.

HIGHS AND LOWS

Joe knew he wanted to serve his community by working as part of the government. He ran for a seat on the New Castle County Council in 1970 and won. Joe served the people of his county well. In fact, some of them wanted him to run for U.S. Senate, even though he wasn't even 30 years old yet!

Joe was elected to the Senate in 1972 and became one of the youngest members of the Senate in U.S. history. However, this exciting news was followed by sadness. Later that year, Joe's wife and daughter, Naomi, were killed in a car accident.

In His Words

"I know how it feels to lose someone you love … I know how mean … and unfair life can be sometimes. But … I found the best way through pain and loss and grief [sadness] is to find purpose."

— Speech given at the 2020 Democratic National Convention

Joe's two sons, Beau (who can be seen here laying down) and Hunter, were badly hurt in the accident that killed their mother and sister. Joe was sworn in as a U.S. Senator at the hospital where they were being treated. Joe has spoken openly about this painful part of his life, and his words have helped many who've lost loved ones.

FAMILY FIRST

Joe had to learn to live with the loss of his wife and daughter while beginning his **career** in the Senate. It wasn't an easy time, and he knew it was hard for his sons too. He wanted to be with them as much as possible. He drove or took the train between Delaware and Washington, D.C., every day he was working so he could spend more time at home.

The Biden family grew again after Joe fell in love with Jill Jacobs. She became Jill Biden after they got married in 1977. In 1981, Jill gave birth to a daughter, Ashley.

In His Words

"No man deserves one great love in his life. But I've known two. After losing my first wife in a car accident, Jill came into my life and put our family back together. She's an educator. A mom. A military mom. And an unstoppable force. If she puts her mind to it, just get out of the way."

— Speech given at the 2020 Democratic National Convention

Joe and Jill support each other in their careers. Dr. Jill Biden has been a teacher for many years. She even kept her teaching job after Joe became president and she became First Lady. No other First Lady had done that before!

MR. VICE PRESIDENT

Joe has always tried to put his family first, but he worked hard in the Senate too. He was a leader in many areas, especially in dealing with other countries and in creating laws that dealt with violence, or bodily harm, against women.

Joe's successful 36 years in the Senate led to a successful 8 years as vice president. He worked in that role, or job, alongside President Barack Obama from 2009 to 2017. During his time as vice president, Joe helped Barack make many important decisions about health care, jobs, and other big issues. He also met and worked with other world leaders.

In His Words

"Jill and I are truly honored to join Barack and Michelle on this journey. When I look at their young children—and when I look at my grandchildren—I realize why I'm here. I'm here for their future."

— Speech given at the 2008 Democratic National Convention

Joe and Jill Biden are shown here with Barack and Michelle Obama on the night in 2008 when Joe was elected vice president and Barack was elected the first African American president of the United States.

13

ENDINGS AND BEGINNINGS

Barack and Joe ended their terms as president and vice president in 2017. However, before they left office, Barack presented Joe with the Presidential Medal of Freedom with Distinction, which is the highest honor the president can give a **civilian**.

Joe took some time after serving as vice president to decide if he wanted to run for president in the future. In 2017, he and Jill started the Biden Foundation to make a difference in many areas, including the fight against **cancer**. Then, in April 2019, Joe announced he was running for president. He was ready to serve his country as a government leader again.

In His Words

"Love is more powerful than hate. Hope is more powerful than fear. Light is more powerful than dark."

— Speech given at the 2020 Democratic National Convention

The fight against cancer is very important to Joe. In 2015, his son Beau (shown with him here) died after a battle with brain cancer.

MAKING HISTORY

One of the most important choices a presidential candidate, or a person running for president, makes is who they want to be their vice president. After serving as vice president for eight years, Joe knew this was an important job, so he wanted to choose the best person for it.

In August 2020, Joe chose Kamala Harris, who was a member of the U.S. Senate at the time. Joe's choice made history. When Kamala became vice president in 2021, she became the first woman—and the first Black person—to hold that position in the U.S. government. She inspired girls and women across the United States.

In His Words

"This morning, all across the nation, little girls woke up, especially little Black and Brown girls who so often feel overlooked and undervalued in our communities, but today … maybe they're seeing themselves, for the first time, in a new way—as the stuff of presidents and vice presidents."

— Speech given on August 12, 2020, presenting Kamala Harris as his choice for vice president

Kamala Harris is making a big difference as vice president, especially for Black girls and women who now can see someone who looks like them in such an important role.

STRAIGHT TO WORK

Joe won the 2020 U.S. presidential election and officially became president in 2021. After becoming president, he went straight to work.

One of the ways presidents can make a difference is by signing executive orders. These are orders straight from the president that act like laws to manage the federal, or national, government. On the day Joe became president, he signed executive orders dealing with issues such as **immigration**, the **environment**, and treating members of the **LGBTQ+ community** fairly. Some of his executive orders dealt with the **COVID-19 pandemic**. Joe wanted to help Americans during this hard time.

In His Words

"I have just taken the sacred [very special] oath … an oath first sworn by George Washington. But the American story depends not on any one of us, not on some of us, but on all of us."

— Speech delivered on January 20, 2021

The Life of Joe Biden

1942
Joseph R. Biden Jr. is born on November 20.

1965
Joe graduates from the University of Delaware.

1966
Joe marries Neilia Hunter.

1968
Joe graduates from law school at Syracuse University.

1970
Joe wins a seat on the New Castle County Council.

1972
Joe is elected to the U.S. Senate; later that year, his wife and daughter are killed in a car accident.

1977
Joe marries Jill Jacobs.

2009–2017
Joe ends his Senate career and serves as Barack Obama's vice president.

2017
President Obama presents Joe with the Presidential Medal of Freedom with Distinction, and Joe and Jill start the Biden Foundation.

2019
Joe announces he's running for president.

2020
Joe chooses Kamala Harris as his vice presidential candidate in August and wins the presidential election in November.

2021
Joe becomes U.S. president on January 20.

Joe Biden has spent most of his life working for the American people in different government roles.

A LEADER FOR HARD TIMES

The U.S. president has to work with the members of the other branches of the government to help the American people. Members of the legislative branch—Congress—make the bills the president signs into law. Members of the judicial branch—the Supreme Court and other courts—make sure laws and executive orders follow the U.S. Constitution.

Joe Biden has spent many years working with other people in the government to get things done. He became president during a hard time, but he knows a lot about living through hard times. He's using those **experiences** to lead Americans toward what he hopes is a brighter future.

In His Words

"One of the most powerful voices we hear in the country today is from our young people."

— Speech given at the 2020 Democratic National Convention

Be Like Joe Biden!

- Run for student government to make a difference in your school community.

- **Encourage** the adults you know to vote for president and other government leaders.

- Write to government leaders about problems in your community or your country that you think they can help solve, or fix.

- Believe in yourself, and take on leadership roles in your class, sports teams, or other groups you're a part of.

- Be respectful of others, and cooperate, or work well, with them on group projects or other tasks.

- Be honest with people you trust when you're going through a hard time, and help other people when they're going through hard times.

- Learn more about the different responsibilities of people who work in the government and different issues that matter to you.

- Raise money for groups that help in the fight against cancer.

You don't have to be the president to make a difference like Joe Biden. These are just a few ways you can get started helping others!

GLOSSARY

cancer: A sometimes deadly sickness in which cells grow in a way they should not, often forming tumors, or growths, that harm the body.

career: A period of time spent doing a job or activity.

civilian: A person not on active duty in the military.

COVID-19 pandemic: An event that began in China in 2019 in which a disease that causes breathing problems, a fever, and other health issues spread rapidly around the world and made millions of people sick in a short period of time.

encourage: To make someone more likely to do something.

environment: The natural world around us.

experience: A life event.

immigration: The act of coming to a country to settle there.

inauguration: The formal gathering to begin a president's term in office.

inspire: To move someone to do something great.

lawyer: A person whose job is to guide and assist people in matters relating to the law.

LGBTQ+ community: A group made up of people who see themselves as a gender different from the sex they were assigned at birth or who want to be in romantic relationships that aren't only male-female. LGBTQ stands for lesbian, gay, bisexual, transgender, and queer or questioning.

responsibility: A duty that a person should do.

FOR MORE INFORMATION

WEBSITES

National Geographic Kids: Joe Biden
kids.nationalgeographic.com/history/article/joe-biden
This website features facts about and pictures of Joe Biden from many different times in his life.

Joe Biden: The President
www.whitehouse.gov/administration/president-biden
The official White House website presents Joe Biden's life story.

BOOKS

Britton, Tamara L. *Joe Biden*. Minneapolis, MN: Abdo Publishing, 2022.

Mikoley, Kate. *Joe Biden*. New York, NY: Enslow Publishing, 2021.

Monroe, Alex. *Joe Biden*. Minnetonka, MN: Bellwether Media, Inc., 2022.

Publisher's note to educators and parents: Our editors have carefully reviewed these websites to ensure that they are suitable for students. Many websites change frequently, however, and we cannot guarantee that a site's future contents will continue to meet our high standards of quality and educational value. Be advised that students should be closely supervised whenever they access the Internet.

INDEX

B

Biden, Ashley, 10
Biden, Beau, 9, 15
Biden, Hunter, 9
Biden, Jill, 10, 11, 12, 13, 14, 19

C

cancer, 14, 15, 21
COVID-19 pandemic, 18

D

Delaware, 6, 10, 19

E

executive orders, 18, 20

G

Gorman, Amanda, 7

H

Harris, Kamala, 16, 17, 19

L

laws, 4, 6, 12, 18, 20

N

New Castle County Council, 8, 19

O

Obama, Barack, 12, 13, 14, 19

P

Presidential Medal of Freedom with Distinction, 14, 19

S

school, 6, 19, 21
speech disorder, 7

U

U.S. Senate, 8, 9, 10, 12, 16, 19

V

vice president, 12, 13, 14, 16, 17, 19